The Fiddler's Tune-Book

JIGS & QUICKSTEPS, TRIPS & HUMOURS

The Fiddler's Tune-Book   Jigs & Quicksteps, Trips & Humours   Copyright © 1997 mally
ISBN 1 899512 49 7

A catalogue in print record for this title is available from the British Library.

Printed by Fretwell Print & Design Limited, Keighley, 01535 600714
Melody arrangements © Folktracks and Soundpost Publications 1967
All music and text artwork © mally 1997
The cover and frontispiece drawing of Charles Benfield of Idbury, Oxfordshire was drawn by A Van Anrooy, RI

mally.com
3 East View, Moorside, Cleckheaton, West Yorkshire, BD19 6LD, U.K.
Telephone: +44 (0)1274 876388
Fax: +44 (0)1274 865208
Web: www.mally.com
Email: mally@mally.com

A mally production

Introduction

The first Fiddler's Tune-Books

THE first two books, of 100 tunes each, were published by Oxford University Press in the early 1950s. At that time they fulfilled a growing post-war need for 'a common language' for musicians and particularly dance bands playing traditional music. In those days I was going round Britain and Ireland collecting local dances and recording fiddlers, pipers and box-players, so I picked those tunes which were the most popular among those particular players. Instead of being in alphabetical order I arranged them according to their usual rhythm: *hornpipe, reel, polka, waltz* and *jig*. At that time, bands playing for barn dances found it especially useful to have similar tune-types on the page next to each other.

Although Oxford University Press sold many copies to musicians playing violins, recorders and other melody instruments, it was undoubtedly because these first two books were used by barn dance bands that ensured their continuing popularity over half a century. So much so that they were much copied and plagiarised without permission, one case involving wholesale photocopying to raise a publisher's collection to a total of 1,000 dance tunes. When questioned, the red-faced plagiarist eased his conscience with the argument that this music "belongs to the people". Quite right it does, but wasn't he forgetting that 'the people' do have certain rights, the moral ones being more relevant than the legal ones? We are thinking here of all the local musicians who had kept the tunes in their memory as well as the many other people involved in the whole process of collecting, recording and publishing traditional dance music for the next generation.

Drops and Raises

In my 1951 introduction to the first book, I wrote about the 'drops and raises' techniques used by traditional dance fiddlers. Questioning those who have copies, I have found that very few owners ever seem to have read the introduction. Perhaps that is the fate of tune-book publishers. However, the first book is still a useful introductory selection of our fiddle tunes and I hope, if you have not yet purchased a copy, at its most reasonable price, you will do so and that you will also take the trouble to read the intro. section on drops and raises.

This expression refers to a specialised technique that was used by the older generation of traditional players, not only on violins, but also on other melody instruments such as flutes, whistles and bagpipes as well as in mouth music for dancing. Of course, this kind of dance music originated in the days when such instruments were played solo, used by themselves for dancing, without the influence of harmony from well-tempered keyboards. Furthermore, these skills were passed on orally from one generation to the next. If tunes were written down, it was only as a reminder, for they were always improvised and developed each time they were played.

Without the restraints of harmonic accompaniment or percussion, the melody itself provided the dance rhythm by means of a variety of tricks of the trade. Listening carefully, sometimes by slowing down recordings, we can detect the little grace-notes or even slides that precede the beat-notes and the general feeling of a held-back strength during the process of letting out percussive bursts of energy. Starting to play, the older players also seemed to move off like a vehicle, from a stationary position, so that they gradually got up to speed, with the greatest control over their acceleration and braking. All these melodic techniques still have their relevance for players today.

Jigs, Quicksteps, Trips and Humours

Many different names were used for the tunes that now go under the generic title of jigs, but at one time had rhythmical significance for certain fashionable dances of their day. Most, at some time, were employed for 'country dances', others, such as *quicksteps* and *gallops*, for 'round dances' and still more were used for 'quadrilles', for which three-part tunes, with the third, or C music, in a minor key, were developed. One also has to bear in mind that probably the majority of our dance tunes started life as song tunes. That is a good reason for our occasionally employing the practice of playing them slowly, more as lyrical song airs. If both players and dancers are familiar with them in this way, then they will definitely play and dance with more enjoyment when they are played at dance tempo.

There is no doubt that our jig-rhythms have an immediate effect on uninitiated listeners, often resulting in their taking a trip into uncontrollable skipping. Therefore, to sustain this rhythm and to provide a little discipline to sustain the dancers, requires some careful handling. Unless we are only giving a short blast, we should avoid going into jigs full belt. We need to recognise that as distinct from the two-beat common-time tunes, often written with dotted notes and requiring straightforward off-beats, we are faced here with, to each main beat, two off-beats of variable values and strengths.

I always try to physically demonstrate this three-beat rhythm as that of sitting on the saddle and holding the reins of a galloping horse. In this way you can appreciate that all three beats will have their own particular place in the scheme of things. As with the two-beat (reels), there must be delay in marking the main (first) beat, but then you have to discover what to do with the two 2nd and 3rd off-beats that make up the *yum-ti-tas*.

Undoubtedly the most valuable piece of advice and we are always saying this about practising traditional music, is: play the tunes at half speed or more. In fact, better advice still is: practice the tunes at continually varying speeds. Start off from the stationary position and then accelerate and decelerate until you have complete control over the rhythm. If you do this, you will find you can really get right inside the tune. Remember that most traditional dance tunes probably started as song airs.

Those experiencing jigs for the first time are likely to be frightened by the number of notes on the paper. That is why I say to players, "Treat them as song airs. Go for the main notes in order to discover the fundamental tune and once you have that mastered, all the other in-between notes will fall into place without your thinking about them". Believe me, it all happens with the help of the subconscious mind. So enjoy your jigs and go for it.

PETER KENNEDY, FOLKTRACKS 1997

The Gloucester Folkatek comprises:

The Folkatek is unique. It is situated in a Georgian terrace in a quiet central city square, adjacent to the docks, with convenient parking; it provides valuable resource and study facilities to many international organisations and interested individuals and to all those concerned with a wide range of traditions in the worlds of education and entertainment;

The Kennedy Collection was built up over four generations of a famous Scottish singing family which included Marjorie Kennedy-Fraser, who collected *The Songs of the Hebrides*; Douglas, who carried on the folk music work begun in England by Cecil Sharp and the Karpeles family, who also worked with Sharp. Peter Kennedy, who started recording in Britain and Ireland in 1950, has built up the most extensive international collection of audio and video recordings. These recordings cover local seasonal customs, children's playground games, singers, storytellers, fiddlers, pipers, box-players and other instrumentalists;

The Reference Library houses over 4,000 specialist books as well as manuscripts, photographs, magazines and journals concerned with oral traditions: anthropology and ethno-musicology, gypsies and tinkers, folklore and language, folk life and folk crafts etc. There is also a well-equipped recording and editing studio, audio and video, using both digital and analogue systems. These facilities are open daily to students and researchers by prior appointment;

Folktracks cassettes, available since 1975, now provide over 300 programmes of authentic field recordings with more items being added to the list every year. Free listings are available or a full catalogue can be purchased for £5·00.

The Kennedy Collection Centre, Reference Library and Folkstudio, Heritage House, 16 Brunswick Road, Gloucester, England, GL1 1UG, telephone 44 (0)1452 415110, facsimile 44 (0)1452 503643, e-mail: folktrax.demon.co.uk

APPLES IN WINTER

(Fruit for Ladies; Gillian's Apples; Jackson's Growling Cat; The Longford Jig; Rise the Grouse; Rouse the Grouse)

THE BALLINA LASSES

THE BARD'S WHYM

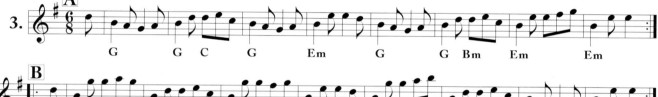

THE BASKET OF OYSTERS

(The Bunch of Currants; The Bunch of Roses; Greensleeves;
I'm a Silly Old Man; The Little Bogtrotter; The Shady Lane; Spring in the Air)

THE BUCK OF TIPPERARY

BUGLE QUICKSTEP NO. 1

BUGLE QUICKSTEP NO. 2

BUGLE QUICKSTEP NO. 3

CAILIN DEAS DONN
(The Big Bow Wow; My Pretty Fair Maid; The Pretty Brown Girl)

14.

THE CAMPBELLS ARE COMING
(Bobbing for Eels; The Butchers of Bristol; The Groom; Jackson's Bottle of Brandy; The Old Man's Jig; Pay the Reckoning)

15.

CAPTAIN BOURN'S FANCY

16.

CASTLEBAR LASSES

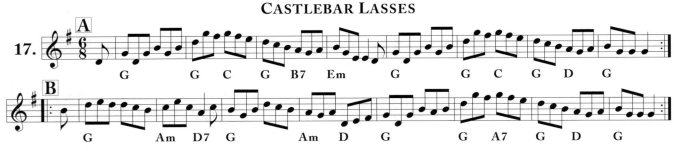

17.

CHERISH THE LADIES
(Capper's Jig; The Humours of Cappa; The Pathway to the Well)

18.

THE CHORUS JIG
(The Kilfenora)

CLOSE TO THE FLOOR
(Father Tom's Wager)

THE COMET

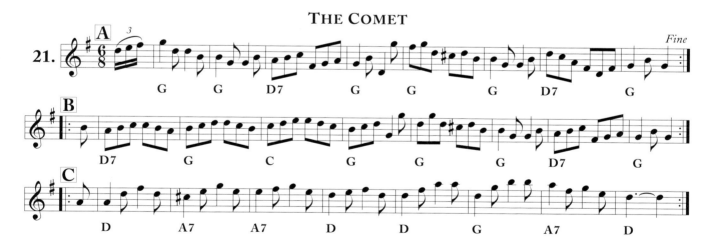

THE CONNAUGHTMAN
(The Humours of Ayle House; The Kilfinane Jig)

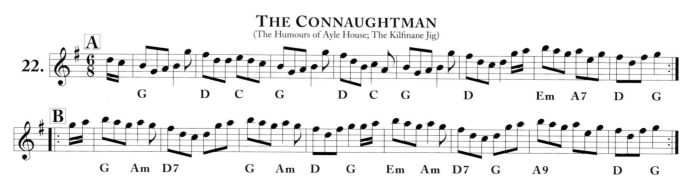

CRABS IN THE SKILLET

CROPPIES LIE DOWN

CROSSMOLINA LASSES NO. 1

CROSSMOLINA LASSES NO. 2

DEVIL OR NO DEVIL

THE DEVIL'S IN DUBLIN

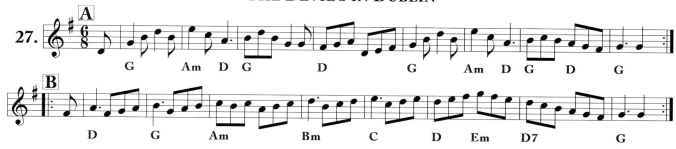

THE DIAMOND JIG

DID YOU SEE MY MAN?

DONAL O'GRADY

(The Bucky Highlander; Daniel of the Sun; Potatoes and Butter; Thady You Gander; You may Talk as You Please)

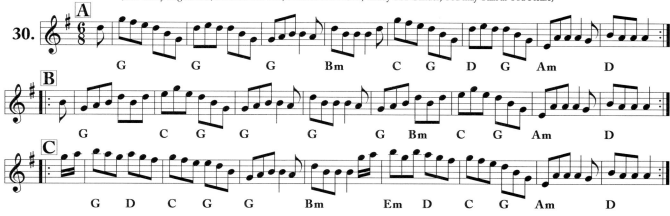

DOURALING

DUNMORE CASTLE

37.

ELLEN ROSENBERG'S FANCY

38.

EPPIE McNABB

39.

FAGAN'S JOURNEY

(Fagan)

40.

FAIRLY SHOT OF HER

41.

GALLOWAY TOM
(Come in the Evening; The Goat's Horn; Kelso Races;
Lark in the Morning; Thrush's Nest; The Welcome; A Western Lilt)

THE GAP IN THE WOOD

GARRY OWEN

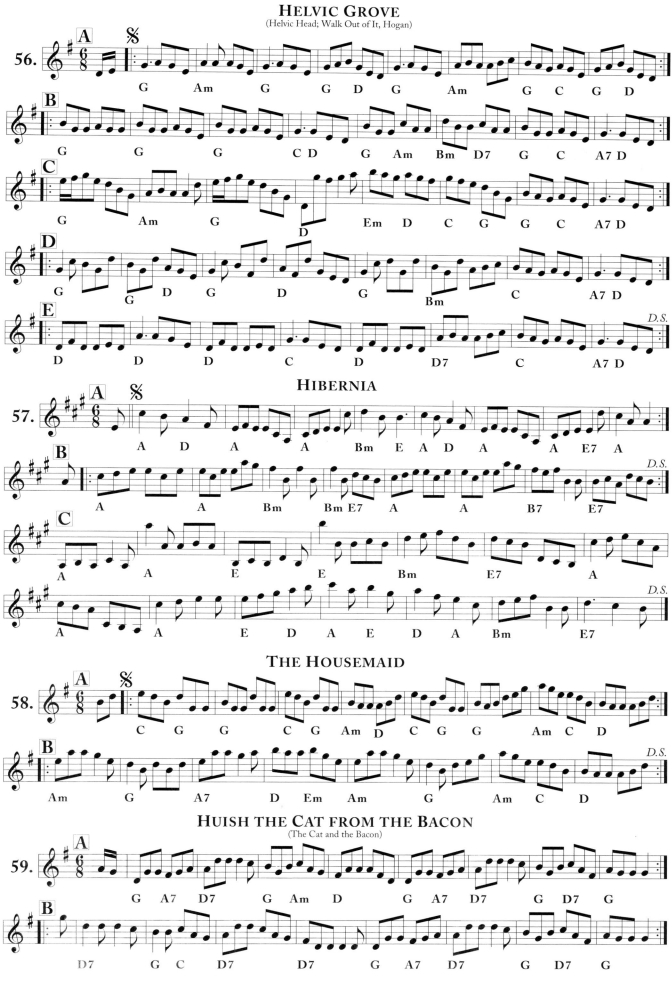

HELVIC GROVE
(Helvic Head; Walk Out of It, Hogan)

HIBERNIA

THE HOUSEMAID

HUISH THE CAT FROM THE BACON
(The Cat and the Bacon)

THE HUMOURS OF ARDNAREE

THE HUMOURS OF BALLINAMULT

THE HUMOURS OF BALTARD

THE HUMOURS OF BANDON
(The Humours of Listivain; The Jolly Old Woman)

THE HUMOURS OF CORK

64.

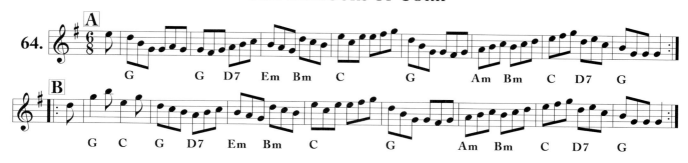

G　　G　D7　Em　Bm　C　　G　　Am　Bm　C　D7　G

G　C　G　D7　Em　Bm　C　　G　　Am　Bm　C　D7　G

THE HUMOURS OF GLIN

65.

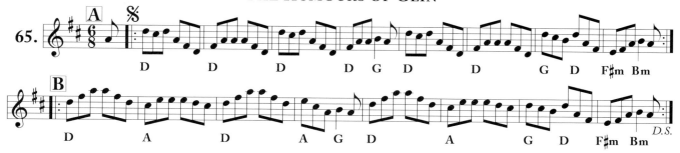

D　　D　　D　　D　G　D　　D　　G　D　F♯m　Bm

D　　A　　D　　A　G　D　　A　　G　D　F♯m　Bm

D.S.

THE HUMOURS OF LAST NIGHT
(Merrily Kiss the Quaker's Wife)

66.

G　　C　　G　　AmD　G　　C　　G　D　C　G

G　　C　　G　　A7　G　　C　G　D　C　G

G　　G　　G　　AmD7　G　　G　　A7　D　C　G

G B7　Em　Bm　A7　　D　　G　D　C　G　A7　D　C　G

THE HUMOURS OF NEWTOWN

67.

Bm A　G F♯m　Bm A　F♯m　　Bm A　Bm F♯m　G D　A

D　　A7　　D　　D　A7　D　　A7　　D　G　A

D　A　G D　D　A　Bm　D　A　G　D　G　A

D　　D　　D　　A　D　　D　　D　G　A

THE HUMOURS OF PASSAGE

THE HUMOURS OF ROSS

THE HUMOURS OF TALLOW

HURRY THE JUG
(Once on a Morning of Sweet Recreation)

IRISH WHISKEY
(Out with the Boys)

JACKEY BULL

JACK IN THE GARRET

JACK'S ALIVE

JACKSON'S BOTTLE OF BRANDY
(Bobbing for Eels; The Butchers of Bristol; The Campbells are Coming; The Groom; The Old Man's Jig; Pay the Reckoning)

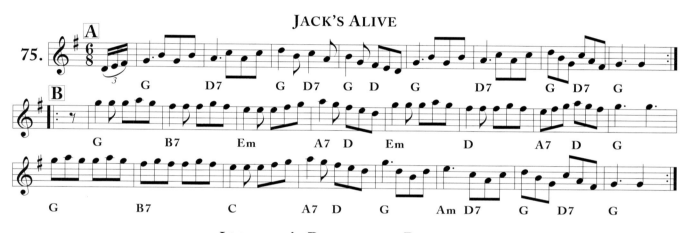

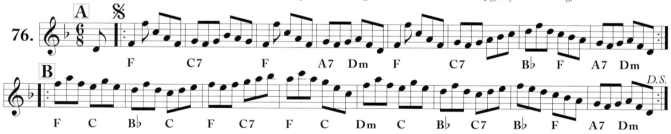

JACKSON'S BOTTLE OF PUNCH

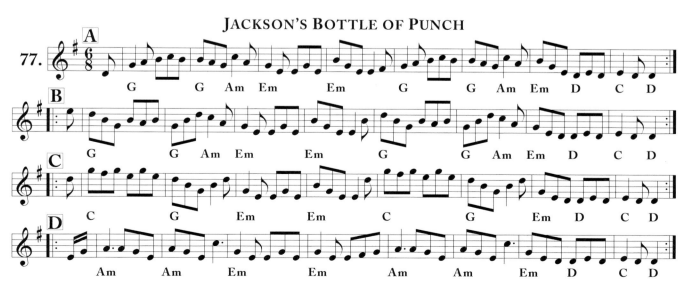

JACKSON'S DAIRYMAID

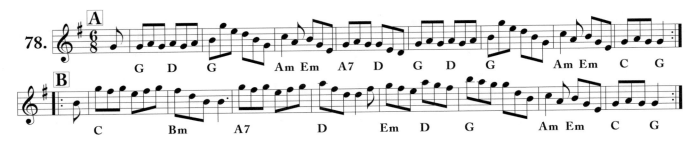

78.

JACKSON'S DREAM

79.

JACKSON'S FANCY

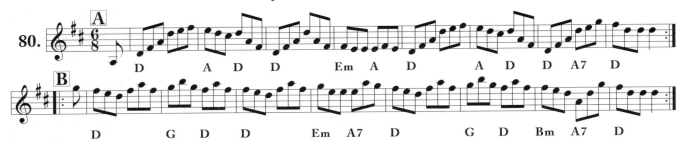

80.

JACKSON'S JIG

81.

JACKSON'S LODGE

82.

JACKSON'S LODGE IN THE MORNING
(Jackson's Coge in the Morning)

JACKSON'S MAID AT THE FAIR

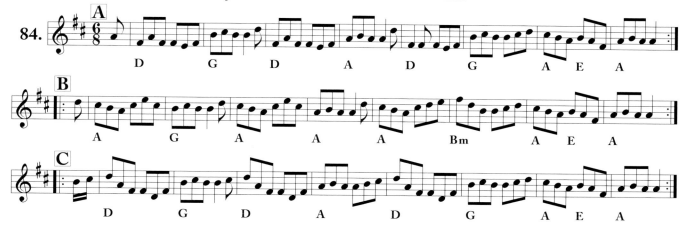

JACKSON'S MORNING BRUSH

JACKSON'S PIPER

JACKSON'S ROWLEY POWLEY

87.

JACKSON'S WELCOME HOME

88.

JOHNNY COCK THE BEAVER

89.

JULIANA

90.

KILLALA MAIDS

91.

KING OF THE PIPERS
(The Kilrane Jig)

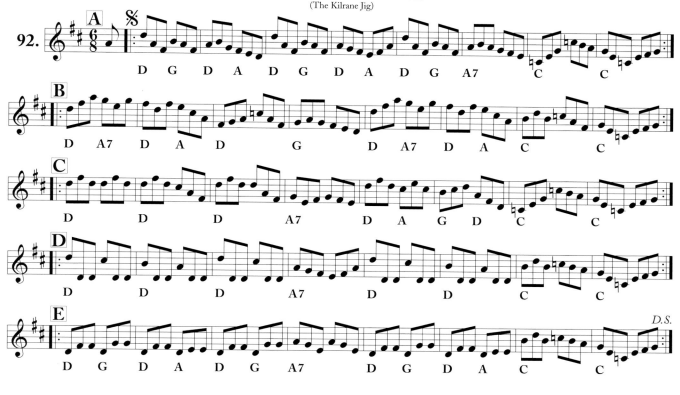

92.

D G D A D G D A D G A7 C C

D A7 D A D G D A7 D A C C

D D D A7 D A G D C C

D D D A7 D D C C

D G D A D G A7 D G D A C C

D.S.

KINLOCH OF KINLOCH
(Blow the Wind Southerley; Yellow John)

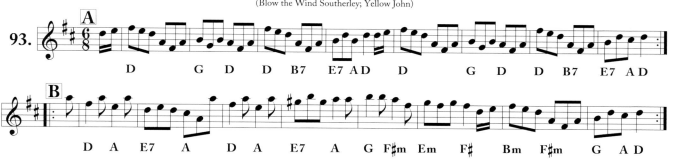

93.

D G D D B7 E7 A D D G D D B7 E7 A D

D A E7 A D A E7 A G F♯m Em F♯ Bm F♯m G A D

KISSING AND DRINKING

94.

D D A7 D G C D D A7 G C A7

C Am F Em C F G C Am F Em G F G

D.S.

THE LAD IN HIS BREECHES

95.

C G C G E7 Am E7 Am C G C G G G

G D C Bm E7 Am E7 Am G D C G G G

D.S.

LADS OF DUNSE
(The Ladds Dance)

96.

LADY SHIRE'S FAVOURITE
(The Happy Mistake; The King of Jigs; Miss Spens Monroe; Rí na bPort)

97.

THE LAIRD O' COCKPEN

98.

LANGSTRAM PONY
(A Draught of Ale; Farrell's Pipes; The Fourpenny Girl; Grania's Welcome Home; The Priest's Leap)

99.

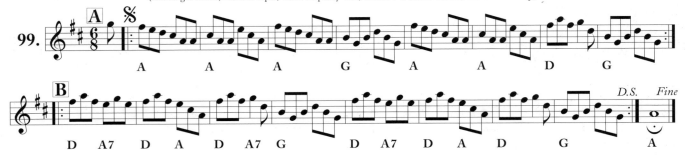

Larry Grogan
(Coppers and Brass; The County Limerick Buckhunt; The Humours of Ennistymon;
Lasses of Melross; Linn's Favourite; Little Fanny's Fancy; The Waves of Tramore)

100.

Larry O'Gaff
(Bundle and Go; Daniel O'Connell)

101.

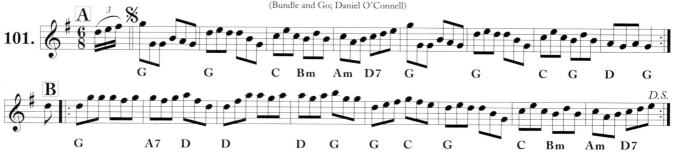

Lasses of Labasheeda

102.

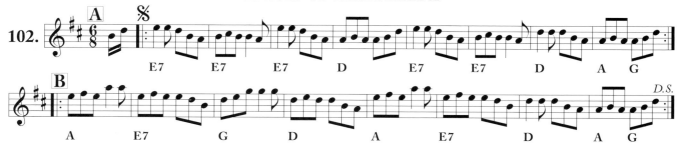

Lasses of Limerick

103.

THE LEGACY

THE LITTLE HOUSE UNDER THE HILL

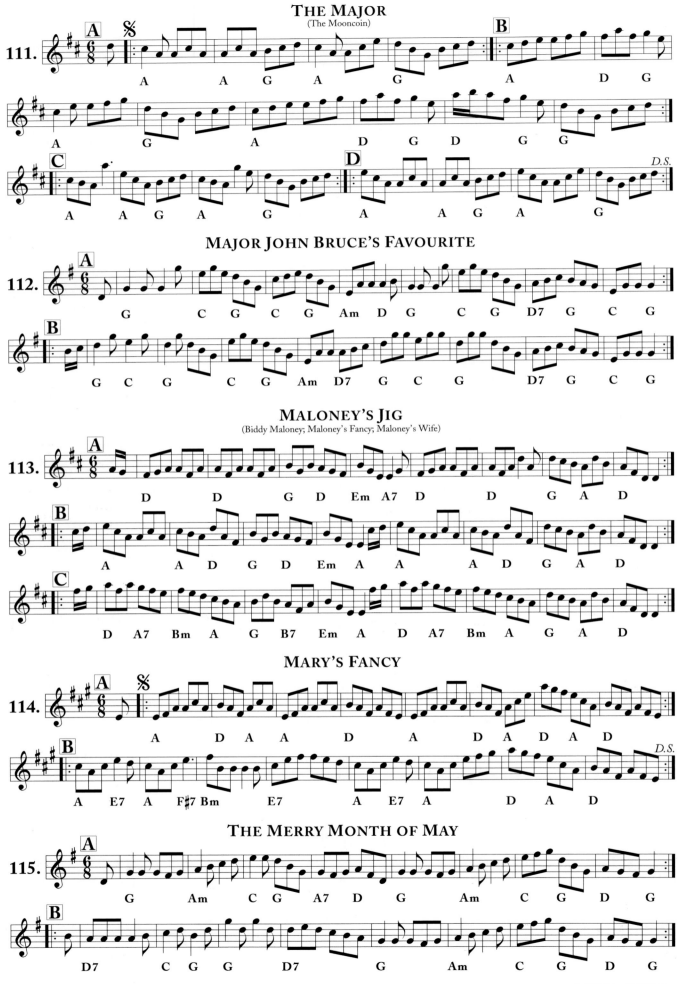

THE MERRY OLD WOMAN

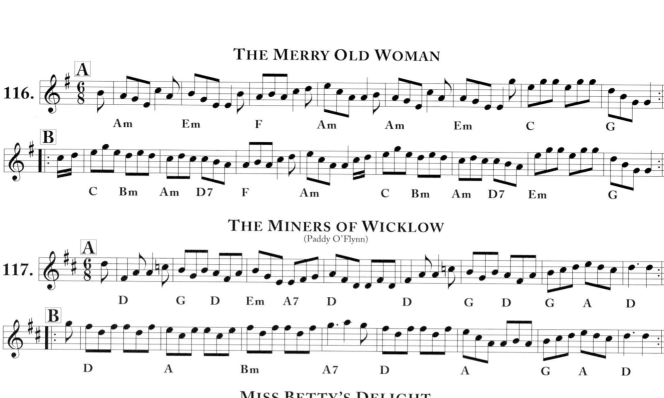

THE MINERS OF WICKLOW
(Paddy O'Flynn)

MISS BETTY'S DELIGHT

MISS GORDON'S FANCY

MRS CASEY
(Billy O'Rourke is the Boy; Billy O'Rourke's the Buachaill; Tá Mo Mhadra)

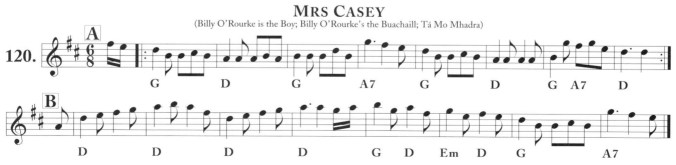

Money in Both Pockets
(Trip to Galloway no. 2)

Morgan Rattler
(Five Hundred a Year; If I had in the Clear; Land of Potatoes)

Morgiana in Ireland
(Morgiana in England)

Mountainy Boys

The Mouth of the Jug

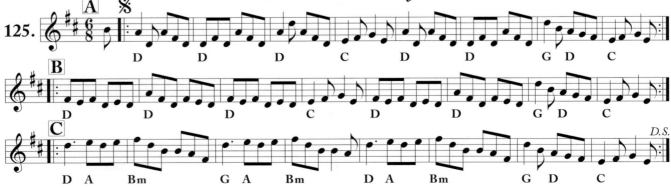

THE MUG OF BROWN ALE
(Old Man Dillon; One Bottle More; The Stonecutter's Jig)

MUNSTER BUTTERMILK
(Barr na Feirste; Behind the Haystack; An Bhláthach Mhuimhneach;
Squeeze your Thighs; Take her or Leave her)

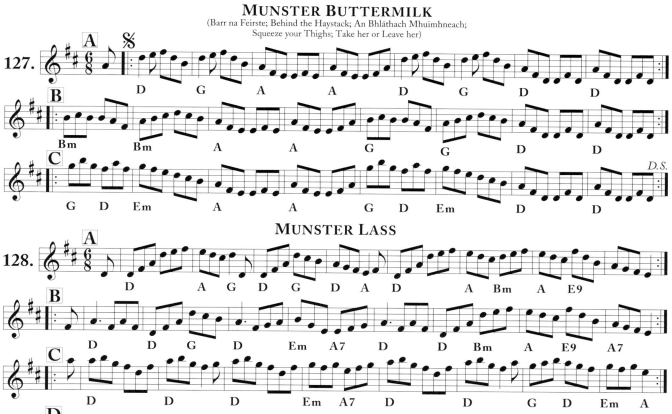

MUNSTER LASS

MURPHY DELANEY

MY PIPES SO SWEET

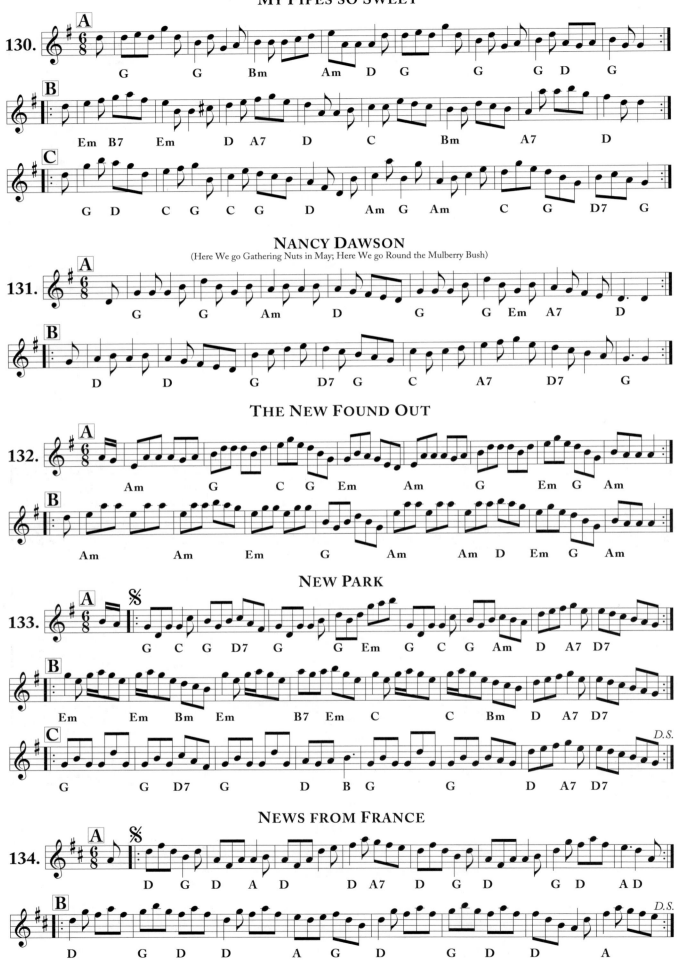

130.

NANCY DAWSON
(Here We go Gathering Nuts in May; Here We go Round the Mulberry Bush)

131.

THE NEW FOUND OUT

132.

NEW PARK

133.

NEWS FROM FRANCE

134.

NEWS FROM PORTUGAL

135.

THE NEWS OF THE VICTORY

136.

NEW TRIP TO THE FERRY

137.

NORA CREINA
(Hushed be Sorrow's Sigh; Lesbia hath a Beaming Eye; Wise Nora)

138.

NORAN KISTA
(Kiss Me, Darling; Maid at the Spinning Wheel; Norah, with the Purse; Norickystie;
The Road to Lurgan; The Spinning Wheel; Tune the Fiddle; The Wild Irishman)

THE OLD WOMAN'S PURSE OF MONEY NO. 1

THE OLD WOMAN'S PURSE OF MONEY NO. 2
(Bill the Weaver; The Humours of Glenflesk; The Lonesome Jig)

ONAGH'S LOCK

PADDY O'RAFFERTY
(Drink of this Cup)

146.

A G D7 G C G D7 G C A7 D

B G G D7 G Em A7 D G G D G Am C D

C G C G G C A7 D G C Bm C Bm A7 D

D G D G G D A7 G D C Bm Em A7 D
D.S.

PADDY THE WEAVER

147.

A F F F A7 Dm F F B♭ C Dm

B F C7 Dm C7 B♭ A7 F C7 Dm C7 B♭ A7 Dm

PADDY WHACK
(The Harp that in Darkness; Tommy Reck's; When History's Muse; Whoop! Do Me no Harm)

148.

A G C G A7 D Em D C G A9 D7 G

B G C G D G A7 D Em Bm C G A9 D7 G

THE PANTHEON DANCE

149.

A G D7 G D G G D7 Em D C G

B G D G A7 D Bm Em C D7 G

THE PARSON IN HIS BOOTS
(Bounce upon Bess; Come all You Good Fellows; Larry O'Lashem;
Paddy's Trip to Dublin; The Priest and his Boots; There are Sounds of Mirth; The Tivoli)

150.

A A A D A E7 A A D A7 D

B D G D A D A7 D G D A D A7 D

PAUL PRY
(No Place Like Home)

151.

A
G Am   Bm   C D7 G   G Am   Bm   C D7 G

B
G   Am   Bm   C   D7 G   C   Bm   Am   D7 G

C
G   Am   Em   D   C   Bm   Am D7 G

THE PEELER AND THE GOAT
(The Bansha Peeler)

152.

A
Am G   Am   Am   G   Am G   F   Em   Am

B
C   Em   Am   G   Am G   F   Em   Am

PIBROCH OF DONALD DHU
(Black Donald, the Piper)

153.

A
A   D   A   A   D   A E   A   D   A   F#m   Bm   A   E

B
A   D   A   A   D   A E   A   D   A   F#m   Bm   A   E
D.S.

THE PLAIN TRUTH

154.

A
Am   Am   G   G   Am   Am   G   Am

B
Am   Am   Em   G   Am   Am   Em G   Am

THE POOR SOLDIER

155.

A
G   C   D   G Em   C   D   G   C   A7   Em   C   D

B
G   G   F   F   G   C D7 G   D7   G

RAYMOND'S FROLIC

161.

RENNY'S FANCY

162.

THE RESOLUTION CUTTER

163.

RORY O'MOORE
(Good Omens; I'll Follow You, My Dear)

164.

ROYAL CHARLIE
(Mulqueeney's; Tiarna Waraga)

165.

THE SAILOR LADDIE

166.

SPIDDLE SPADDLE

172.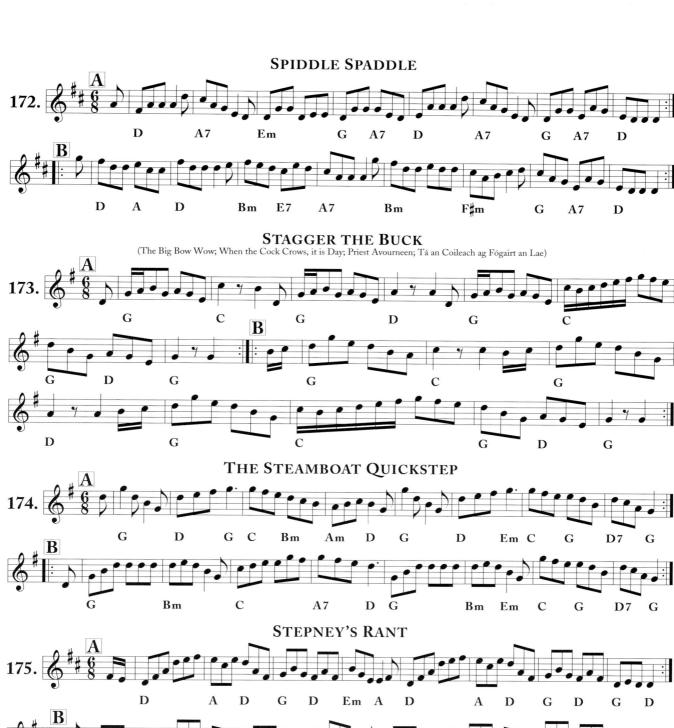

STAGGER THE BUCK
(The Big Bow Wow; When the Cock Crows, it is Day; Priest Avourneen; Tá an Coileach ag Fógairt an Lae)

173.

THE STEAMBOAT QUICKSTEP

174.

STEPNEY'S RANT

175.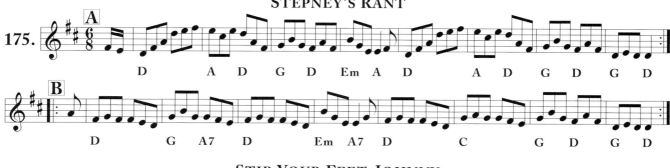

STIR YOUR FEET, JOHNNY
(Keep Your Feet, Johnny; The Northern Road)

176.

D.S.

THE STONY ROAD

177.

STRAYAWAY CHILD

Composed by Margaret Barry © Folktracks Publications 1956

178.

STROP THE RAZOR

179.

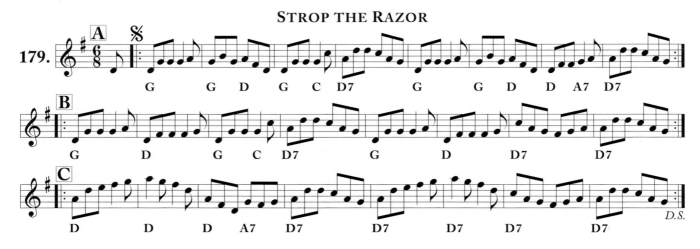

THE SWALLOW'S NEST

(The Dancing Master; Dromey's Fancy; From the New Country; The Swallow Tail Jig)

180.

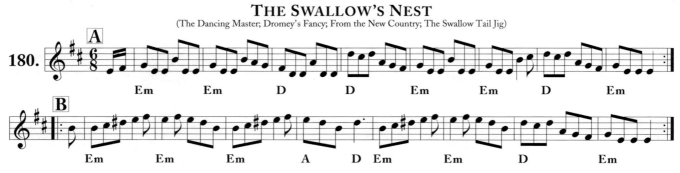

THE TRIP TO KILLARNEY

187.

TRIP TO THE FERRY

188.

THE TURNPIKE GATE

189.

TWO-MILE BRIDGE

190.

THE UNFORTUNATE RAKE

(The Basket of Turf; Bundle and Go; An Cliabh Móna; The Disconsolate Buck;
The Lass from College Land; Wandering Harper; The Wee Wee Man)

191.

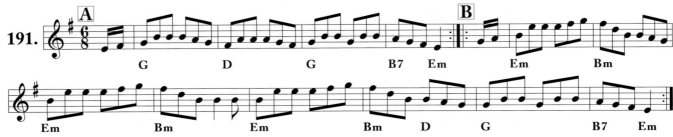

WATTY'S FANCY

192.

WELSHMAN FROM WENS

193.

WHISKEY AND BRANDY

194.

THE WICKED COOK

195.

WIDOWS ALONE

196.

WILD IRISHMAN

(Kiss Me, Darling; Maid at the Spinning Wheel; Norah, with the Purse; Noran Kista;
Norickystie; The Road to Lurgan; The Spinning Wheel; Tune the Fiddle)

WILD OATS

WILLY'S FANCY

THE YELLOW WATTLE

(The Ladies' Fancy)

ALPHABETICAL INDEX TO TUNES

Alternative titles are shown in *italics*